EDGE OF MEDICINE

MEDICAL
ROBOTICS
BREAKTHROUGHS

T0015889

HEATHER E. SCHWARTZ

MAYO CLINIC PRESS KIDS

To Philip, Jaz, and Griffin

MAYO CLINIC PRESS KIDS | An imprint of Mayo Clinic Press
200 First St. SW
Rochester, MN 55905
mcpress.mayoclinic.org
To stay informed about Mayo Clinic Press, please subscribe to our free e-newsletter at mcpress.mayoclinic.org or follow us on social media.

For bulk sales to employers, member groups and health-related companies, contact Mayo Clinic at SpecialSalesMayoBooks@mayo.edu.

Proceeds from the sale of every book benefit important medical research and education at Mayo Clinic.

ISBN: 978-1-945564-81-9 (paperback) | 978-1-945564-80-2 (library) | 978-1-945564-82-6 (ebook) | 979-8-88770-086-1 (multiuser PDF) | 979-8-88770-085-4 (multiuser ePub)

Library of Congress Control Number: 2023934470
Library of Congress Cataloging-in-Publication Data is available upon request.

TABLE OF CONTENTS

MEDICAL ROBOTS
AT WORK

Grace is ready to care for her patient. "I will take your temperature reading with this little **thermal** camera on my chest, see?" she explains. "You're 97.8 degrees Fahrenheit."

What may appear to be an average interaction between a nurse and a patient is actually a medical marvel. Grace is not a human nurse—she's a robot! Scientists released the robot nurse in 2021 to aid doctors in caring for patients during the **COVID-19 pandemic**.

Robots have been at work in health care since the mid 1980s. Today, more and more robots are at work in medical settings. These devices provide therapy and patient care and even complete **surgeries**.

Scientists and engineers are continually improving technology to create advanced robots. Many modern medical robots are also lifelike—some even seem **sentient**!

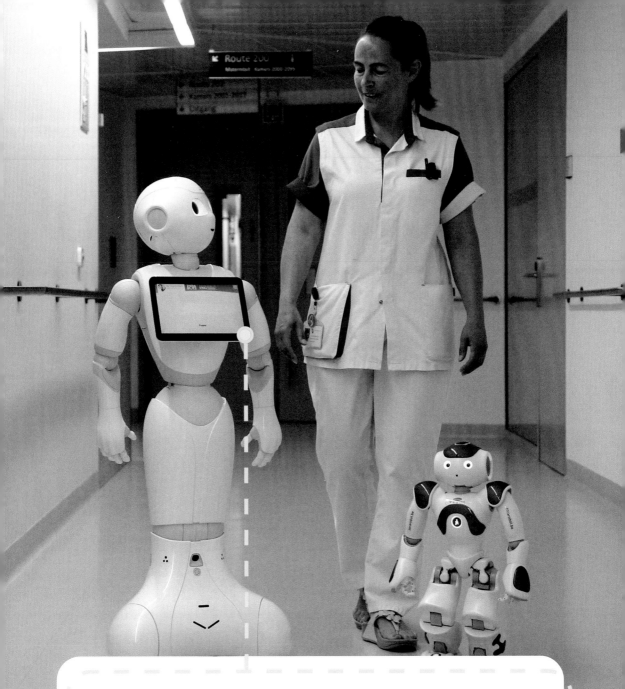

Robots work in hospitals around the world! Robots Pepper (*left*) and Zora (*right*) are on duty with a human nurse in a Belgian hospital. The robots care for patients and communicate with hospital visitors.

ROBOTIC EXOSKELETONS

In the late 1960s, researchers at the Mihailo Pupin Institute, in modern day Serbia, had an idea. They wanted to create a wearable robot that could assist people who had trouble walking. They got to work creating an **exoskeleton**.

Led by engineer Miomir Vukobratovic, the Mihailo team built an exoskeleton powered by **pneumatics**. Mihailo performed more than 100 **clinical trials** of the exoskeleton. Many partially **paralyzed** patients learned to walk using the device with the assistance of crutches!

Mihailo's work was inspiring. But available technology of the time kept the exoskeleton from being recreated to successfully sell. For decades, researchers and engineers kept hard at work improving robots.

Advancing technologies led to the creation of the EksoNR in 2019. This was Ekso Bionics' third updated version of an exoskeleton. It helps people experiencing trouble walking due to injury. EksoNR gets them moving, which reteaches their brain and muscles what to do. Over time, some patients may still need help walking, but others can eventually do so without assistance!

Dale Messenger (*left*) wears the Ekso GT in 2017 in Germany. The Ekso GT was a previous version of the EksoNR. A main update to the newer version was the inclusion of a touchscreen controller.

ROBOTS IN
SURGERY

The year was 1985. A patient needed a brain **biopsy**. Doctors prepared the surgery needle. But the doctors wouldn't be the ones to **insert** it into the patient's brain. A robot named PUMA 560 would!

With a robot on the job, there was no chance of error from shaky hands. PUMA 560's successful biopsy was the first time a robot assisted with surgery. This began an era of exploration and invention in medical robotics.

After PUMA, engineers built more robots to assist in surgery. One was ROBODOC, released in 1992. It could make exact movements more quickly than human surgeons could. ROBODOC helped doctors place a patient's artificial hip in California.

Eight years later, a company called Intuitive Surgical released the da Vinci Surgical System. The system has helped perform more than 10 million surgeries since its creation! It is used in hospitals around the world.

A patient at Mayo Clinic in Minnesota in surgery with the da Vinci Surgical System. The clinic began offering various robot-assisted surgeries in 2018. By 2022, collective US Mayo Clinics performed over 4,000 robotic surgeries each year!

The da Vinci system moves like a human hand but is much tinier. Surgeons control the robot through a viewing **console**. The system allows them to enter the body through tiny **incisions**. Smaller incisions can heal faster.

Scientists continue to improve surgical robots. The robotic surgeons of the future may be smaller, faster, and more precise than ever imagined!

ANIMAL THERAPY
ROBOT

Does snuggling a baby animal sound comforting? Japanese doctor Takanori Shibata thought so when he created PARO. It is a robotic baby harp seal made to improve the lives of senior citizens with **dementia**.

Shibata began his work on PARO in 1993. He knew dementia was a leading cause of death and disability among the world's elderly. Memory loss caused by dementia makes people living with the disease often feel alone. Research had proven caring for a pet can provide connection. But it isn't safe for dementia patients to interact with real animals that can scratch and bite. Real pets also need people who can remember to care for them.

Enter PARO! Shibata released PARO in 1998. It can recognize voices, wiggle its tail, and squeak. It responds when stroked. PARO can even learn to move in response to someone saying its name!

By 2015, PARO was being tested in senior care facilities worldwide. Researchers studied its interactions. They found PARO makes patients feel happy. It also inspires staff to talk more often with their patients. This creates not only human to PARO connections, but human to human ones too.

Residents at a retirement center in Japan in 2011 spend time with PARO robots. The robotic seals contain microphones, sensors, and processors that power their reactions.

PILL-SIZED
ROBOTIC CAPSULE

Diagnosing **gastrointestinal** problems can be uncomfortable for patients. The exam includes having an **endoscope** inserted into their body. But endoscopes don't fit in one section of the small intestine. This area also can't be seen with an **X-ray**. So, some patients must have diagnostic surgery. Israeli inventor Gavriel Iddan wanted to change this.

Iddan released his invention, the PillCam, in 2001. It is a robotic **capsule** outfitted with a camera. The PillCam is given to a patient to swallow. Inside the patient's body, the device takes photos and sends them to a special device the patient wears on a belt. This endoscopy is done in a clinic, without the need for hospitalization. And it is pain-free!

The PillCam led to ideas for more advances. Since 2019, scientists at the Korea Institute of Medical Microrobotics have been working on their own robotic capsule. It will perform endoscopies. The scientists hope it will also collect **tissue** and **inject** medicine directly into organs.

After an endoscopy using the PillCam, patients pass the swallowed device in a bowel movement!

BIONIC
BODY PARTS

The first **prosthetic** arms were invented beginning in the 1500s and made of iron and springs. Centuries later, inventors in the 1900s made prosthetics powered by pneumatics. By the 1980s, Scottish engineer David Gow believed he could further improve prosthetics. He turned to robotics!

Gow led a team to develop the Edinburgh Modular Arm System in 1988. Made of metal and plastic, it weighed 3.96 pounds (1.8 kg). This was lighter than any previous prosthetic arm.

Electronic parts inside the device sent **pulses** to the arm. Miniature motors created movement. The arm's exterior was covered with artificial skin. The device blended mechanical and realistic parts. It was the world's first **bionic** arm!

In 1998, Campbell Aird was the first to wear Gow's invention. The arm changed Aird's life! He took up piloting and won trophies for clay pigeon shooting.

Gow's invention spurred new research in bionic prosthetics. And Gow himself continued inventing bionics. In 2007, he

Campbell Aird models his bionic arm in 1998, five years after receiving it. Doctors had amputated Aird's biological arm in 1982 to prevent muscular cancer from spreading to the rest of his body.

revealed the iLIMB, a bionic hand. Each finger had its own tiny motor. This allowed the wearer to move fingers individually. The technology was the first of its kind.

KELLIE L. MATHIS, MD

MAYO CLINIC

Q: When did you first become interested in robotics?

A: I first became interested in robotic surgery in 2010 when I was a trainee in surgery. Robotics was new to my field of surgery (colon and rectal), and I was fascinated by this new technique. I participated in many additional learning courses and eventually began to use the robot in the operating room.

Q: What is the most exciting thing happening in medical robotics today?

A: There are many different companies developing new robots that can help with surgeries in all parts of the body, from the mouth to the abdominal organs and even the joints. It is fun to see what the new robots can offer.

Q: How can robotics help doctors perform more successful surgeries?
A: Robotic surgery allows surgeons to perform operations through tiny incisions instead of big ones, which helps our patients recover faster. They also allow magnification and 3D visualization of the organs inside the abdomen.

Q: What is the most rewarding part of working in medicine for you?
A: I LOVE meeting new patients and their families, and it is an honor for me to be a part of their care journeys.

Q: What might the future of robotics in medicine look like?
A: I think that robotics is here to stay. The technology will continue to advance, and we will find more and more uses for the robot in surgery and in medicine. It is an exciting time to be a doctor!

THE FIRST ROBOT
PHARMACIST

Pharmacists handle many tasks. They interact with patients, check and fill **prescriptions**, and can provide **vaccines**. In 1990, US student Sean McDonald wanted to help busy pharmacists do their jobs. McDonald was studying the way industries complete their work. He thought robots could help pharmacy processes!

McDonald began working on an **automated** prescription drug **dispenser**. His ROBOT-Rx could select, store, and restock drugs. It also kept records of dosages. It is important pharmacists perform these tasks correctly to avoid giving a patient the wrong drug or drug amount. ROBOT-Rx prevents the possibility of human error. The robot had 99.9 percent **accuracy** when performing its tasks. By 2001, ROBOT-Rx had filled 45 million prescriptions without a single mistake!

In addition to preventing errors, the ROBOT-Rx also freed up pharmacists' time. This allowed them to spend more time on important interactions with patients and doctors.

The ROBOT-Rx at work. Doctors order medications, and pharmacists review these orders and enter them into computers. Then the ROBOT-Rx reads barcodes to identify, count, and package the medications.

PRACTICE CARE ON A
CHILD ROBOT

HAL is a five-year-old boy. He can answer a doctor's questions and track a doctor's finger with his eyes. When HAL gets scared, he breathes faster. Though all these actions are human, HAL is not. He's a robot!

Researchers and engineers at Gaumard Scientific in Florida created **Pediatric** HAL. The robot provides medical teams training for pediatric patients. HAL was given humanlike qualities so this training resembles real life as closely as possible.

HAL can make facial expressions. He has a pulse. His artificial organs make realistic sounds. HAL can even bleed fake blood! These features allow medical workers to treat HAL the way they would a human child. This helps prepare the workers for real patients.

When HAL was released in the 2010s, he was the world's most advanced pediatric patient **simulator**. His lifelike simulations raised safety standards for medical training.

A version of Pediatric HAL. The robot underwent updates between its release and 2018. Each version had software that allowed HAL to be connected to certain medical support devices. The software provided data realistic to that of human patients.

DELIVERY ROBOTS IN
HUMAN CELLS

In 2018, University of Texas student Soutik Betal developed robots so small they could not be seen by the human eye. His goal for the bitty bots? To enter human cells! Betal hoped the tiny devices would **deliver cancer** treatment drugs directly into patients' cells.

Cancer is often deadly. But cancer treatments exist, and scientists work to improve them. Betal's robot idea was one improvement. It would improve the cancer treatment **chemotherapy**. Current chemotherapy delivery methods kill both cancer cells and healthy cells. This causes patients to feel very ill. Betal's bots would enter only cancer cells, leaving healthy cells alone!

Scientists are using robots to address other chemotherapy issues too. It takes time and many steps to prepare treatment sessions. In 2022, Minnesota's Mayo Clinic Cancer Center installed a robotic **intravenous** compounding system. It prepares chemotherapy treatments quickly and correctly. This allows

A digital illustration shows how tiny robots could perform various tasks in a human body. The robot at top left injects chemotherapy drugs into a cancer cell, the task Soutik Betal hoped his invention would complete!

nurses to focus on patient comfort and care. The robotic system also saves time, meaning more cancer patients can be treated!

HUMANLIKE
CARE COMPANION

Sometimes elderly adults living alone feel lonely in their homes. Maybe their family and friends can't visit very often. And leaving the house can be difficult for elderly people who no longer drive or walk easily. Loneliness can affect a person's mental health.

Intuition Robotics in Israel wanted to help treat senior loneliness. In 2017, it released ElliQ. The robot was built to be a humanlike companion to seniors. ElliQ answers when spoken to. But she can also start a conversation. She offers greetings, reminders, and suggestions for movies and music without being asked. ElliQ's ability to start interaction is important for seniors who are withdrawn due to mental illness.

In 2019, several ElliQ robots were delivered to the Center for Aging and Brain Health Innovation in Toronto, Canada. Studies are still in progress to prove whether ElliQ helps its seniors feel less alone. But those testing the robot already agree the answer is "yes."

ElliQ gets to know its user better with each interaction. The robot remembers bits of information as the user talks. ElliQ uses this stored information to tailor future conversations and suggestions. This creates a personalized experience.

HUMANOID
ROBOT NURSE

Grace is a **humanoid** nurse. Hanson Robotics in Hong Kong launched the robot in 2021. At this time, health care workers were very busy caring for patients during the COVID-19 pandemic. Grace could be cloned to provide extra nurses.

Staff shortages weren't the only pandemic problem Grace solved. To help stop COVID-19's spread, people were ordered to stay home and away from others. Nurses could catch the disease from patients, and patients from nurses. But Grace could interact with people without the risk of spreading the disease!

The care Grace provided was similar to that from human nurses. She could detect a patient's temperature and pulse. Grace could talk in three languages: English, Mandarin, and Cantonese. During conversation, motors placed beneath Grace's artificial skin allowed her to make expressions in reaction to patients' words or phrases.

The head and neck of Grace, with her electronic components exposed, sit beside an engineer at Hanson Robotics. The robot's head will later be fitted with hair and attached to a robotic body.

Even as the pandemic came to an end, nursing shortages remained a problem. And researchers estimate 1.2 million new nurses will be needed by 2030 to care for the growing population. Grace is designed for the job. Maybe she'll care for you in the future!

TIMELINE

LATE 1960s

The Mihailo Pupin Institute develops the first medical robotic exoskeleton. It inspires future exoskeletons.

1988

Engineers begin working on the world's first bionic arm, the Edinburgh Modular Arm System. The device debuts ten years later.

2000

The da Vinci Surgical System is released and soon used in hospitals worldwide.

1985

PUMA 560 assists in surgery. It's the first time a robot performs this task.

1998

PARO, a robotic baby harp seal, is developed. It provides therapeutic care to people with dementia.

2001

PillCam is developed to perform endoscopies. It leads scientists to develop robotic capsules with even more capabilities.

2010s

HAL is the world's most advanced pediatric patient simulator.

Tiny robots are developed that could deliver cancer treatment directly to patients' cells.

2017

Intuition Robotics develops ElliQ, the first humanlike care companion for seniors.

2021

The humanoid robot Grace launches. She helps care for patients during the COVID-19 pandemic.

GLOSSARY

accuracy—the degree to which something is free from mistakes or error

automated—completed with little or no human assistance

bionic—an electronic or mechanical device replacing something natural

biopsy—the removal of tissue, cells, or fluids in order to check for illness

cancer—a group of often deadly diseases in which harmful cells spread quickly

capsule—a small case that typically holds one dose of medicine

chemotherapy—the use of chemicals to treat or control a disease

clinical trial—a study done to see how efficient and safe a new or emerging treatment is

console—an electronic system that connects to a screen

COVID-19 pandemic—a global spread of the SARS-COV-2 virus beginning in early 2020

deliver—to send or bring. This action is called delivery.

dementia—a mental illness that causes someone to be unable to think clearly or to determine what is real

dispenser—a device that gives things out

endoscope—an instrument introduced into the body to give a view of its internal parts. This procedure is called an endoscopy.

exoskeleton—a rigid external covering

gastrointestinal—related to the system of organs that take in food and liquids and break them down for the body's use

humanoid—looking or acting like a human

incision—a cut made into the body during surgery

inject—to force a liquid medicine or drug into someone or something for medical purposes

insert—to place something into another thing

intravenous—being in or entering through a vein

paralyzed—unable to move or function

pediatric—relating to the branch of medicine that cares for infants and children

pneumatic—using air pressure to move or work

prescription—a doctor's written order for a medicine

prosthetic—an artificial body part

pulse—a beat, vibration, or burst of current or energy that occurs in a rhythm. Contractions of the heart cause a rhythmic ejection of blood and are detected as a pulse.

sentient—able to sense or feel

simulation—something that is made to look, feel, or behave like something else. A machine or device used in this process is called a simulator.

surgery—a medical treatment performed on internal body parts. This treatment is performed by a surgeon.

thermal—relating to heat

tissue—a group of like cells that work together in the body to perform a function

vaccine—a medication prepared and given, often by injection, to protect a person against a disease

X-ray—an image taken using radiation and showing a portion inside the human body

LEARN MORE

How to Be Good at Science, Technology, and Engineering. London: DK Children, 2018.

Laperia, Raúl, and Andreu Marsal. *The Maker's Guide to Building Robots: A Step-by-Step Guide to Ordering Parts, Using Sensors and Lights, Programming, and More*. New York: Sky Pony Press, 2019.

National Geographic Kids: Could a Robot Become President?
https://kids.nationalgeographic.com/books/article/could-a-robot
-become-president

PBS Kids: Design Squad Videos—Rescue Robot
https://pbskids.org/video/design-squad-nation/1642106856

INDEX

PHOTO ACKNOWLEDGMENTS

David Cheskin/Alamy, p. 15; Ekkasit919/iStockphoto, cover (robotic machine in surgery); Erik Viktor/Science Source, p. 23; FRANCOIS LENOIR/REUTERS/Alamy, p. 5; Gannet77/iStockphoto, pp. 13 (bottom), 29 (top); Intuition Robotics, pp. 25, 29 (bottom); Jens Meyer/AP Images, p. 7; Kim Kyung Hoon/Alamy, p. 11; kynny/iStockphoto, cover (child and robotic machine); Mayo Clinic, pp. 9, 16, 28; onairp/Shutterstock Images, back cover; PhonlamaiPhoto/iStockphoto, cover (humanoid robot); Sakurra/iStockphoto, p. 13 (top, center); traffic_analyzer/iStockphoto, cover (background); Tyrone Siu/REUTERS/Alamy, p. 27; Viacheslav Onyshchenko/SOPA Images/Sipa USA/AP Images, p. 21; vijay0401/Shutterstock Images, cover (abstract sprocket); ZUMA/Alamy, p. 19